CRAWSHAW'S WATERCOLOUR STUDIO

CRAWSHAW'S WATERCOLOUR STUDIO

ALWYN CRAWSHAW

HarperCollins*Publishers*

in association with
Channel Four Television Corporation
and Teaching Art Ltd

ACKNOWLEDGEMENTS

I would like to express my grateful thanks to all the members of the television film crew for their tremendous support during the making of *Crawshaw's Watercolour Studio* and, in particular to the director, David John Hare.

I would also like to record my sincere thanks to Cathy Gosling from HarperCollins, to Flicka Lister for editing this book, and also to Gertrude Young and Mary Poole for typing my almost unreadable manuscript.

Finally, as always, I am indebted to June, my wife, who didn't appear in front of the television cameras in this series, but worked just as hard behind them on my behalf.

The eight-part television series, *Crawshaw's Watercolour Studio*, was produced by Teaching Art for Channel Four. Videos of the series are available from Teaching Art Ltd, P O Box 50, Newark, Notts NG23 5GY.

Unless otherwise stated, the close-up details in this book are reproduced actual size.

First published in 1993 by
HarperCollins Publishers
London

Reprinted 1993

© Alwyn Crawshaw, 1993

Edited and typeset by Flicka Lister
Designer: Joan Curtis

Photography: Nigel Cheffers-Heard

Alwyn Crawshaw asserts the moral right to be identified as the author of this work.

All rights reserved. No part of this publication may be reproduced, stored in a retrieval system, or transmitted, in any form or by any means, electronic, mechanical, photocopying, recording or otherwise, without the prior written permission of the publishers.

A catalogue record for this book is available from the British Library

Jacket photograph of the author by
Nigel Cheffers-Heard

ISBN 0 00 412943 1

Printed and bound in the UK

CONTENTS

PORTRAIT OF THE ARTIST	6
INTRODUCTION	8
MATERIALS	10
Watercolour	10
Gouache	13
Acrylics	14

PROGRAMME 1
PAINTING THE SEASONS — 18

PROGRAMME 2
SMALL SKETCHES — 28

PROGRAMME 3
USING PHOTOGRAPHS
PEN AND WASH — 36

PROGRAMME 4
PAINTING SKIES — 44

PROGRAMME 5
USING IMAGINATION — 54

PROGRAMME 6
CREATING ATMOSPHERE — 60

PROGRAMME 7
IN THE GARDEN
USING GOUACHE — 70

PROGRAMME 8
PAINTING LANDSCAPES
USING ACRYLICS — 76

GALLERY — 84

PORTRAIT OF THE ARTIST

Successful painter, author and teacher Alwyn Crawshaw was born at Mirfield, Yorkshire, and studied at Hastings School of Art. He now lives in Dawlish, Devon, with his wife June, where they have their own gallery. As well as painting in watercolour, Alwyn also works in oils, acrylics and occasionally pastels. He is a fellow of the Royal Society of Arts, and a member of the Society of Equestrian Artists and the British Watercolour Society. Alwyn is also President of The National Association of Painters in Acrylics.

Alwyn's best-selling book *A Brush with Art* accompanied his first Channel Four television series in 1991. *Crawshaw Paints on Holiday* and *Crawshaw Paints Oils* were his second and third Channel Four television series with tie-in books of the same titles. This book, *Crawshaw's Watercolour Studio*, accompanies his fourth Channel Four television series.

Alwyn's previous books for HarperCollins include eight in their *Learn to Paint* series, *The Artist at Work* (an autobiography of his painting career), *Sketching with Alwyn Crawshaw*, *The Half-Hour Painter*, *Alwyn Crawshaw's Watercolour Painting Course* and *Alwyn Crawshaw's Oil Painting Course*. His forthcoming book in 1994 is *Alwyn Crawshaw's Acrylic Painting Course*.

Alwyn has been a guest on local and national radio programmes and has appeared on various television programmes. He has made several successful videos on painting and in 1991 Alwyn was listed as one of the top ten video art teachers in America where his television programmes have been screened. He is also a regular contributor to *Leisure Painter* magazine.

Alwyn organises his own successful and very popular painting courses and holidays, as well as giving demonstrations and lectures to art groups and societies throughout Britain. He has also co-founded the Society of Amateur Artists, of which he is President.

Fine art prints of Alwyn's well-known paintings are constantly in demand. His paintings are sold in British and overseas galleries and can be found in private collections throughout the world. Alwyn has exhibited at the Royal Society of British Artists in London, and he won the prize for the best watercolour on show at the Society of Equestrian Artists' 1986 Annual Exhibition. He is listed in the current edition of *Who's Who in Art*.

Painted mainly from nature and still life, Alwyn's work has been favourably reviewed by critics. *The Telegraph Weekend Magazine* reported him to be 'a landscape painter of considerable expertise' and *The Artist's and Illustrator's Magazine* described him as 'outspoken about the importance of maintaining traditional values in the teaching of art'.

INTRODUCTION

Welcome to my studio.

This is the book of the fourth television series I have made. In the previous three television series, I mainly painted outdoors. Here, I am working indoors and my intention is to show you how to develop your watercolour painting skills and to encourage you to try your hand at some other water-based mediums like gouache, pen and wash and acrylics.

Many leisure painters frequently work at home, especially in the winter when the weather is not always ideal for painting outside. In the television series and in this accompanying book, I hope to teach, inspire and encourage you to paint watercolours indoors. I will also be sharing my painting experiences with you and giving you practical painting tips.

Watercolour is the ideal medium to work with in your own home. You don't need much equipment, nor do you need an enormous room to work in. Your 'studio' can be the kitchen table, or a small table in the corner of any room. Indeed, some people work with their pad on their knees, so you could even manage with just a chair and a jar of water on the floor.

I remember, when I first started painting as a boy, that I used to kneel or sit on the floor, but I've rather outgrown that now! And my first *real* studio was a tiny corner of my attic bedroom where there wasn't much space because the eaves sloped right down to the floor. But it was my very own private place and I painted many pictures there.

I have a large studio now and my paintings are better – but only through experience, not just because I work in a large, well-lit studio. So, you don't have any excuses. Remember, even if your studio is only a corner of the kitchen table, you can still paint a masterpiece!

Keep practising your watercolour painting and, as you do, you'll gain more confidence and will get more pleasure out of your work.

Good luck and *enjoy* your painting!

Alwyn Crawshaw

MATERIALS
WATERCOLOUR

Each artist's choice of materials is, of course, a very personal matter and, when you have gained experience, you will be ready to make your own decisions. In the meantime, if you are a beginner, I suggest you use what I use. In addition, to get the best results, you should use the best-quality materials you can afford.

COLOURS

There are two types of watercolour paint, which differ in both quality and cost. The top quality ones are called artists' watercolours and the other ones, which are a grade lower, are called students' watercolours, some of which are manufactured under brand names such as Daler-Rowney Georgian Watercolours. You can buy watercolour boxes filled with paints, or empty and ready to fill with your choice of colours. My large box, shown opposite, holds 12 pans, but I often use just the six colours shown above and these were the only colours I used in the television series.

Watercolour paint also comes in tubes but I don't advise beginners to use these: the strength of the pigment and the soft consistency of the paint when squeezed out on to the palette can make it difficult to control the amount of paint picked up by the brush. So, for beginners, I recommend Daler-Rowney Artists' Watercolours (whole or half pans) in a watercolour box.

BRUSHES

It isn't easy to place colours, brushes and paper in order of importance but I feel that brushes must come out on top. Brushes make the marks with which we create paintings and which type of brushes we use and how we apply the paint with them determines individual style.

For watercolour painting, there is only one general-purpose brush that a traditionalist would use: a round sable. When you use a sable brush, you are following in the brush strokes of the Old Masters, although I must add that to paint like them there must also be a little magic in the hand that holds the brush! These brushes, which last for years, are at the top of the price range but man-made fibres are now successfully used to replace the sable hairs in artists' brushes, making them far less expensive. Sold under brand names such as the Daler-Rowney Dalon series, many professional artists use these for all their watercolour work.

For me, the main difference between synthetic and sable brushes is water-holding ability. Synthetic brushes only hold about two-thirds as much water as sable, and I love using bags of water when I paint! However, I find the smaller sizes of these brushes excellent for detail work. The three brushes shown below are, in fact, the **only** brushes I use for all my watercolour painting.

FROM THE TOP: Dalon rigger; No. 6 round sable; No. 10 round sable

• MATERIALS •

| Crimson Alizarin | Cadmium Yellow Pale | French Ultramarine | Cadmium Red | Yellow Ochre | Hooker's Green No. 1 |

My large paintbox holds 12 whole pans but I normally use only six colours

My basic watercolour kit

Paper

Which paper should you choose? Traditionally, the three different surfaces used for watercolour are called Rough, Hot Pressed and Not. Rough means the surface is rough; Hot Pressed (HP) means the surface is very smooth; and Not (sometimes called Cold Pressed or CP) indicates that the surface is in between rough and smooth – by far the most commonly used. The weight or thickness of paper is determined either by grams weight per square metre (gsm) or by calculating how much a ream of paper (500 sheets) weighs. So, if a ream weighs 300 lb (about the heaviest you can use), the paper is so called (with its manufacturer's name and surface type), for example, Waterford 300 lb Not. A good weight of paper to work on is 140 lb (285-300 gsm).

In the television series, I used Bockingford, Whatman and Waterford watercolour paper, cartridge drawing paper, and tinted Bockingford watercolour paper. The paper I used is named under each painting. Bockingford watercolour paper doesn't have a surface title, being made with only one surface, but it has different weights and is an excellent, inexpensive paper. Cartridge paper has only one surface and the weight doesn't vary much; the cartridge paper I use in sketchpads is 70 lb (150 gsm). The other papers are traditional ones with three different surfaces and different weights and these are slightly more expensive than Bockingford or cartridge paper.

The secret of finding the right paper to work on is to try out different ones until you discover which suits you best. Then use it, practise on it and get to know it. A good art supply shop will sell these papers in pads of various sizes, or in sheets, usually 51 x 76 cm (20 x 30 in). I find that cartridge paper is lovely for painting small sizes, say up to 28 x 41 cm (11 x 16 in) and I suggest you get a sketchpad of this paper. It is also the paper commonly used for drawing.

Basic Kit

The basic materials you need to start watercolour painting in the studio are shown above. 'Basic' does not refer to their quality but to the minimum quantity necessary to enable you to follow the television series. As you gain experience, you can build up this basic kit to suit your own needs. All you need is a paint box to hold a minimum of six paints, whole or half-pan size; three brushes: a No. 10 and a No. 6 round sable, or a No. 10 and a No. 6 Dalon (synthetic), and a Dalon Series D99 'Rigger' No. 2 (the very thin one); a 2B pencil for sketching; a putty eraser; a water jar; and paper on a drawing board or a pad. I normally work on a table indoors but, if you prefer to use an easel, go ahead.

• MATERIALS •

Gouache

Crimson | Cadmium Yellow (hue) | Ultramarine | Cadmium Red | Viridian

Leaf Green | Burnt Umber | Yellow Ochre | Geranium | Permanent White

Colours

Gouache paints come in tubes and there are many colours available – the Rowney Designers' Gouache range that I use has 90 different colours. So when you gain experience and want to experiment with ready-mixed colours, there will be plenty to choose from! However, I suggest that, as with watercolour, you start with a limited palette and learn to mix colours first.

The colours I used for the painting in the programme were: Crimson, Cadmium Yellow (hue), Ultramarine, Cadmium Red, Viridian, Leaf Green, Burnt Umber, Yellow Ochre, Geranium and Permanent White.

Brushes

I used my three watercolour brushes but if you want to experiment with hog brushes (used for oil and acrylic painting) or synthetic (Dalon), then please do. There are no hard-and-fast rules!

Paper

You can use any of the watercolour papers, Ingres paper or board, available in many different colours. On television, I used tan Ingres board.

Palette

You can use a dinner plate (many artists do) or buy a plastic or ceramic palette. The round plastic palette below is the one I used for the television series.

My plastic gouache palette

13

• MATERIALS •

ACRYLICS

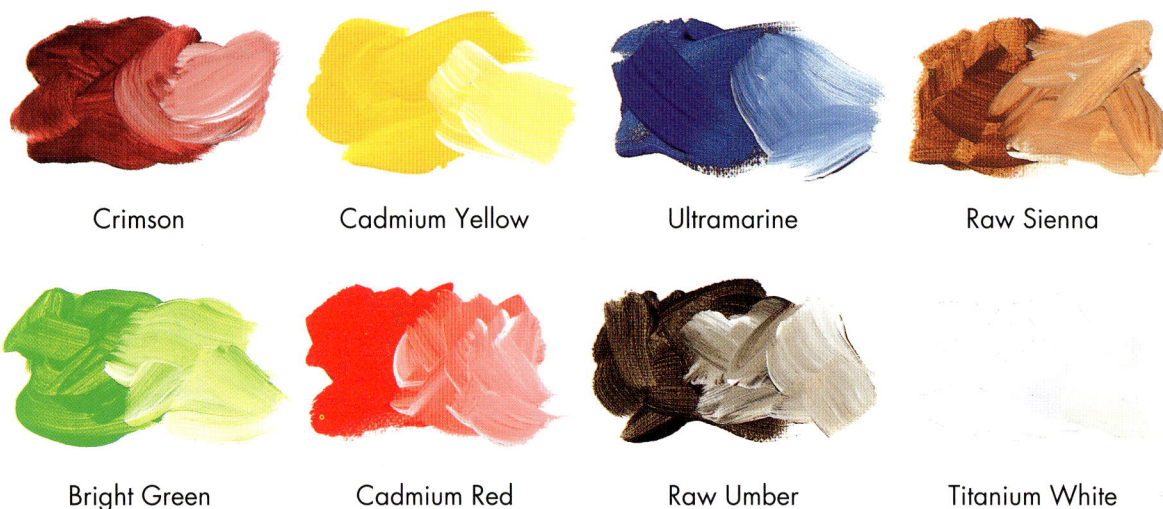

Crimson Cadmium Yellow Ultramarine Raw Sienna

Bright Green Cadmium Red Raw Umber Titanium White

COLOURS

The acrylic colours I used for the television series are shown above. These are all Daler-Rowney Artists' Cryla Flow Colours, which have a consistency similar to gouache and come in tubes. Daler-Rowney also make another type of acrylic paint called Cryla Colour which is thicker and has a more buttery consistency than Cryla Flow Colour – when you're shopping for colours, don't get the two confused! Cryla Colour is ideal for work with a palette knife but can naturally be used with a brush and I love using it to add more texture to my paintings.

If you haven't used acrylic colour before, my advice is to start painting with **only Cryla Flow** until you have more experience, then try the thicker paint and see if you gain anything extra from it. I only use Cryla Colour for about five per cent of any painting – mainly to give texture to foreground – but sometimes I don't use it at all.

I use just seven colours and white, and from these I can mix all the colours I require. If you would like to experiment with others, then do, but a word of caution. The more ready-mixed colours you use, the longer it will take you to learn how to mix colours. Finally, replace the caps on the tubes or your paint could dry out.

BRUSHES

The range of brushes available for acrylic painting is vast. You can use most traditional oil painting brushes – these are made from hog bristle and come in various sizes with different shapes of bristle. You can also use synthetic (Dalon) and sable brushes. Obviously, as you gain experience, you will want to experiment with different types of brushes but, to get started, I suggest you choose from the ones I use:
Bristle brushes: I use Daler-Rowney's Bristlewhite Series B36.
Synthetic brushes: I use Daler-Rowney's Cryla Series C25, which is made specially for acrylic painting, and a Dalon Series D99 'Rigger' (the same brush I use for small detail in my watercolour and gouache painting).
Sable brushes: I use my small watercolour brush. (See Basic Kit for brush sizes.)

PAINTING SURFACES

There are many painting surfaces (grounds) on which to work. You must make sure that the surface is free from oil or grease, and if the surface is too absorbent for you, then it must be primed with an acrylic primer (gesso). If you use an oiled

My basic acrylic kit

primed canvas, then you must always over-prime it with acrylic primer.

Although I used a canvas when I did my painting in Programme Eight, there is a far less expensive surface which I recommend you use. Cryla Primed Paper is made specially for acrylic painting and is ideal for the purpose. It is supplied in spiral-bound sketchbooks of varying sizes, ranging from 50 x 40 cm (20 x 16 in) down to 17 x 13 cm (7 x 5 in).

PALETTE

I can only recommend one palette – the Daler-Rowney Stay-Wet Palette. If you follow the instructions, your paints will keep wet almost indefinitely and it will save you a lot of paint!

BASIC KIT

The picture at the top of the page shows you the materials you will need to start painting in acrylic. I used an easel for my painting in Programme Eight, but you can rest your work against the back of a kitchen chair, or buy a small table easel, to start with. If you work on acrylic primed paper rather than an expensive canvas, you won't need acrylic primer. My basic kit is only a guide, so you can always feel free to add materials of your choice. However, remember that the fewer materials you work with, the easier it will be for you to learn to paint in acrylic!

The colours you will need are the ones recommended on the opposite page. Your brushes should be either the Bristlewhite Series B36 Nos. 8, 4 and 2, or the Cryla Series C25 Nos. 12, 8 and 4, plus a Dalon Series D99 'Rigger' No. 2, and a round sable No. 6.

You will need a Stay-Wet Palette and a Cryla sketchbook or a support of your choice; a pencil, plastic eraser; some rag; a water jar; a brush dish and a tube of Gel Retarder. When mixed with paint, this helps to slow down the drying time of paint on the canvas (if you feel it is necessary). I only use Gel Retarder for large sky areas, where I am working wet-on-wet paint.

The 8 Programmes

Painting The Seasons

2

Small Sketches

3

Using Photographs

4

Painting Skies

A course of easy-to-follow watercolour painting lessons to accompany the television series

Using Imagination

Creating Atmosphere

7

In The Garden

8

Painting Landscapes

PROGRAMME

PAINTING THE SEASONS

There are many reasons for painting in the comfort of your own home. The most obvious is, of course, the weather. You can't do a watercolour outside in the rain and, in the winter, it is often too cold to work out of doors. Even in the summer, if you live in a city but love to paint landscapes or seascapes, it isn't always convenient to travel to your subject. But there can be rewards, and many masterpieces are born at home in the studio, the spare room or on the kitchen table. In fact, many beginners prefer to work at home first, simply to learn how to paint before they go out to work in the public eye.

One of the greatest assets of working at home or in the studio is that it gives you time to prepare and to really think about what you are painting. When you work outdoors time is often against you. Anything can happen, whether it's an approaching rainstorm, something suddenly blocking your view, or your subject moving – the boat that looked a permanent fixture in the harbour can move away in minutes, leaving you artistically high and dry. Or you may simply run out of time or daylight. At home, you are in control of the elements, which makes it easier to concentrate on your painting.

If you want to paint landscapes or seascapes, you must try to do some work outdoors from nature if possible, since this is where you will learn at first hand about your subject.

Pencil sketches can be tremendously useful because sketching helps to train your powers of observation and visual memory. The amount of work put into a sketch is up to the individual. You are gathering information to work from at a later date when your real subject won't be there

I sketched this scene for television

to help you, and some students need to draw in far more detail than others. You can make colour notes on the back of your sketch. I never write all over a pencil sketch, as I might decide to paint over it at a later date. A photograph of the scene can also help if you use it with your sketch when you are working at home.

One pencil sketch can be used for many different paintings in the studio. For this programme, I did the sketch opposite out of doors, with the object of painting three different seasons from the one sketch back in the studio. The most important part of the sketch was positioning the largest tree and the cottage. I felt that the odd-looking tree on the left of the biggest tree was not going to help the sketch at all. It was too solid, and its shape was very uninteresting, so I left it out. I didn't try to draw every branch on the trees either, but concentrated on the overall shape. The shading I did was sufficient to give me the tonal values that I needed and I took a photograph as well.

2B pencil on cartridge drawing paper, 20 x 25 cm (8 x 10 in)

The most important part of the sketch was the positioning of the largest tree and the cottage

SKETCHING TIPS

Observation is the key word to good sketching

Make sure you're comfortable when you are sketching

Make colour notes on another piece of paper, or lightly on the back of your sketch

Always draw enough information on your sketch to work from back home

SPRING

The first season I used my sketch to paint from was spring. I felt that the sky should play a major part in creating the illusion of spring, and so I gave more space to the sky and less to the foreground. This is something I often do when working from sketches.

I painted a blue sky with plenty of white, wind-blown clouds (see Programme Four: Skies). I also put a dark shadow, cast from the clouds, over part of the field in the middle distance. This helped to give the illusion of a windy, sunny day.

I purposely painted the field in front of the cottage in a bright 'spring green' wash, leaving some white paper showing through to give the freshness and sparkle which we associate with springtime. The large trees have a wash of warm green over them to suggest budding leaves.

Look at the dark shadow on the left side of the cottage. I left the right hand part as white paper to show strong sunlight. In the foreground, I painted shadows coming from the large trees.

Please note when colour mixing that the first colour I specify in the main text or under **'Important Colours'** *is usually the main colour of the mix, with the other colours being added in smaller amounts.*

IMPORTANT COLOURS

The spring greens
Hooker's Green No. 1 with a touch of Cadmium Yellow Pale. I added a little touch of Crimson Alizarin to this mix for the budding leaves on the trees

The blue sky
French Ultramarine, with a little Crimson Alizarin

The shadow of the clouds
The same colours as the sky, using Yellow Ochre for the sunlit areas

---

▶ Watercolour on Whatman 200 lb Rough, 28 x 38 cm (11 x 15 in)

• PROGRAMME ONE •

WINTER

I love to paint snow scenes, especially in watercolour. When your flowing brush strokes capture the sparkle of snow in the fields, it's quite a magical feeling! I talk in more detail about this in Programme Five.

To help give the illusion of winter for this painting, I made two important decisions. Firstly, to enable me to show more snow, I decided to have more landscape than sky; quite the opposite of the springtime painting. Secondly, I would paint a dark winter sky, which would contrast against the white of the snow and help to give the snow more importance. Because the horizon has been moved high up in the painting to give less sky, the tops of the main trees are not in the picture. In fact, it is amazing that the scene changes so much simply by moving the horizon.

When painting, always be conscious of tonal values and remember that a dark tone against a light tone or vice versa will give strong contrast. In this painting, I have made the old gatepost in the foreground dark against the light snow because a light-coloured post would have disappeared. In the autumn painting on page 24, I made it light-coloured, to show up against the darker background. Remember – light against dark or dark against light will help to make objects stand out and be 'readable' in a painting.

Finally, I made the main tree darker at the bottom of its trunk, contrasting with the white unpainted paper left for snow. The eye is led to this because of the strong contrast and this helps to stabilise and give strength to the painting.

> **IMPORTANT COLOURS**
>
> **The sky**
> French Ultramarine, a little Yellow Ochre and a touch of Crimson Alizarin
>
> **The snow shadows**
> French Ultramarine, Crimson Alizarin and a touch of Yellow Ochre

▶ Watercolour on Whatman 200 lb Rough, 28 x 38 cm (11 x 15 in)

AUTUMN

For this painting, which I did for television, I worked from the sketch with my 2B pencil without making any alterations. I painted the sky with a wash, starting at the top and working down into the fields (see Programme Four: Skies). As soon as this was dry, I painted the distant trees on the top of the hill. When you do this, paint your brush strokes vertically, see Fig. A. I used my No. 6 sable and any underpainting that is left showing appears as vertical lines and looks sympathetic to growing trees. You will also find that this brush stroke, when started at the top, gives a good shape to the tops of distant trees. If you use horizontal brush strokes, your trees could look as though they have been cut in half.

You will see two types of arrow in all the demonstration photographs in this book. The solid black arrow shows the direction of the brush stroke, and the outlined arrow indicates the direction in which the brush is travelling over the paper, working from top to bottom or bottom to top.

I painted the main group of trees with my No. 6 sable and rigger brushes, working from the bottom of the tree upwards in the direction that the tree grows or the branches go. I worked the trunk and main branches with my sable, then put in the small branches with my rigger brush. You can use your rigger for thin and thick branches. If you want a thick stroke (your paint must be watery) press the brush on its side, flattening the hairs. This gives a broad stroke. To get a thinner stroke, take the pressure off the hairs and keep the brush more upright, as shown in Fig B. Practise this brush stroke – you will find it quite easy to master and it will help you to paint good trees. I painted the right-hand tree this way.

When the trees were dry I painted the mass of small, feathery branches with free brush strokes, working over the trunk and branches and adding autumn colours for leaves that were still on the trees. You can see that I put more strength of colour at the foot of the trees and in the hedge.

When I painted the foreground field, I left areas of white paper unpainted for puddles of rainwater and, while the field paint was still wet, added a warm blue over these white puddle areas, letting the wet paint touch the wet field in places to soften the edges. Where I didn't touch, you can see some lovely sparkling white paper left and this helps to give the illusion of wetness. I wanted the atmosphere of a day in late autumn and that's why I put the puddles in. I always think of this time of the year as wet and damp!

I made the field in the middle distance a ploughed one, so that the autumn colouring would be very prominent, and I painted the hedge on the left quite solidly, as I didn't want it to be too fussy and stop the eye from going on in the picture to the trees and cottage. I painted over the main trees again when they were dry, leaving some underpainting showing to represent weak sunlight falling on the tree.

Incidentally, I didn't have time to paint a summer scene on television, but the painting shown on pages 2 and 89 is one I did from a pencil sketch I made five years earlier.

IMPORTANT COLOURS

The sky
French Ultramarine and a little Crimson Alizarin, adding more water and yellow Ochre and a little more Crimson Alizarin to the mix as you work down. Add Hooker's Green No. 1 as you go into the fields

The autumn field and trees
Crimson Alizarin, Yellow Ochre, Cadmium Yellow Pale and a little French Ultramarine

The main trees
French Ultramarine, Crimson Alizarin, Hooker's Green No. 1 and Yellow Ochre

The puddles
The same as the sky colours

Watercolour on Bockingford 200 lb, 28 x 38 cm (11 x 15 in)

Fig. A

Fig. B

CLOSE-UP DETAILS

▶ Leaving unpainted paper on the right side of the cottage contrasts with the left side which is in shadow and gives the cottage a three-dimensional appearance. It also helps to suggest sunlight

▶ The water for the puddles was painted in while the field colour was still wet. Allowing two wet colours to touch in places blends the colours and softens the edges. Where the paint does not touch and a white edge (paper) is left, it gives a crispness to the area

▲ When you are out, screw up your eyes and look at a tree. The mass of small branches (the feathery ones) will show only as a tonal area, not as individual branches. I suggested this here by painting 'free' brush strokes of watery colour over the existing painted branches

▼ Look how simply I painted these trees – they were done with a single 'wash'. If trees are in the middle distance, they don't need to be any more detailed than this

▶ Simplicity is the keynote of this sky and the middle distance. You can see how the wash for the sky was worked from left to right across the paper by the start of each brush stroke on the left edge of the paper

PROGRAMME

2

SMALL SKETCHES

The second programme in the series also found me gathering information to be worked from at home, but this time we went to a much busier location. The spot we chose was Turf Lock on the Exe estuary in Devon and, for an artist, this place seems to have everything! There's a canal which is separated from the estuary by a lock; yachts and boats moored on the canal, and even an old inn by the lock with all sorts of interesting bits and pieces that help to make up a very paintable scene. In addition to this, behind the inn, the mud of the estuary gives way to the rising tide. Beyond, on the other side of the river, the town of Topsham and its neighbouring villages straddle the water's edge and fields rise up behind them, finishing with a strong skyline silhouetted against the sky.

Have you ever been out for a day's sketching and, when you've reached the spot, felt it looked so vast and complicated, or had so much to choose from, that your creative energy has instantly dried up? Well, every problem has a solution! If you are confronted with a scene like this and, either because you are intimidated by it – we've all felt like this at some time – or you simply feel like relaxing and don't want to tackle a big subject, then do as I did. I decided to sketch small areas that inspired me as I wandered around enjoying the general scene. It was also very windy and it would have been difficult to sit in one place for any length of time.

I drew the Victorian light on the side of the inn because it was the first thing that inspired me. Next, the wrecked barge in the mud was an exciting find. The life belt caught my eye later and so that went into my sketchbook, too. Doing these three sketches gave me a great deal of pleasure. They are references to use at home in future paintings and they made me practise – something we **all** need to keep doing! Finally, they gave me something that I could frame, or just keep in my sketchbook for occasional walks down memory lane.

▲ This life belt made an interesting small sketch

▶ 2B pencil on cartridge, 28 x 20 cm (11 x 8 in)

• PROGRAMME TWO •

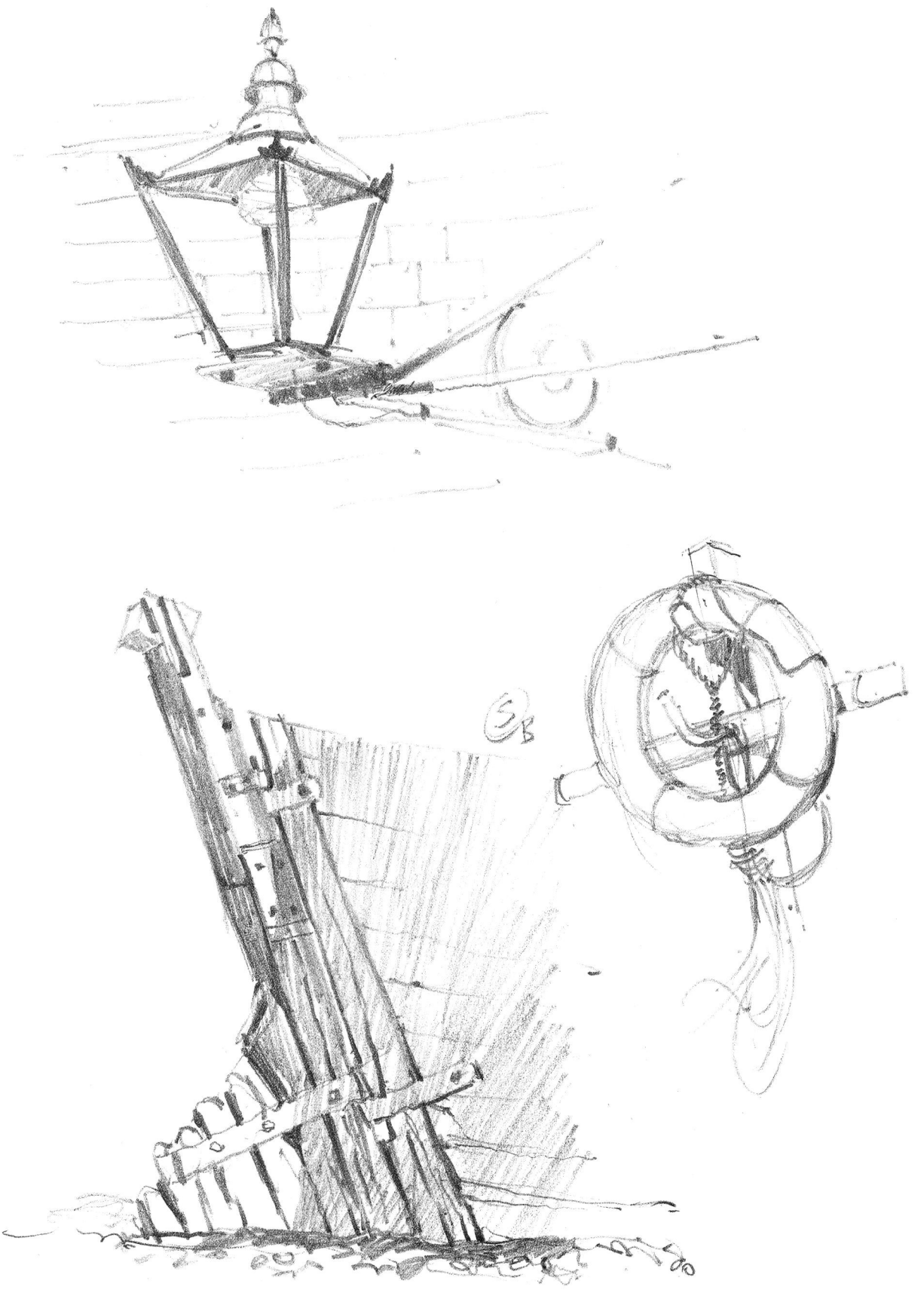

• PROGRAMME TWO •

I drew the yacht on page 33 next on television, and then the view over the estuary, opposite, but I'll discuss the estuary first. While we were outside having lunch, I was looking across the estuary and a shadow went over the distant trees. This formed a silhouette on the skyline which contrasted with the sunlit houses and the blue water of the estuary. I was inspired! With the sun lighting up everything on the other side of the estuary for miles, the subject hadn't been very interesting. However, with a small part of it transformed by sunlight and shadow, it really became a little gem.

Always look out for small areas in a vast panorama. I did the sketch very freely and it didn't take me long. I put the yacht in to add a little life to the painting. Back at the studio, I painted it very freely, but I made sure I painted the small group of trees (top left) carefully as they are an important landmark. When you work over a small pencil sketch like this, keep your colour mixing simple. I made sure that the sky was dry before I painted over the silhouette of the trees on the hills. The detail below is reproduced twice the original size to show you just how simply you can work. This is important. In fact, if you tried to paint everything carefully, I don't think a painting like this would work.

Detail from my painting (*right*), reproduced twice the size that it was painted

2B pencil and watercolour on cartridge, 12 x 17 cm (5 x 7 in)

▲ My view of the estuary

▶ Paint water with horizontal brush strokes, so that any underpainting or paper that shows through accidentally or by design gives the impression of moving water

2B pencil on cartridge, 11 x 20 cm (4½ x 8 in)

While I was enjoying wandering about, I spotted this yacht, and the bright blue of its canopy and windblown clouds behind it really whetted my artistic appetite! It proved quite difficult to sketch because the wind kept blowing my sketchpad, but I sat on a bollard, which helped to steady me. Always try to make yourself as comfortable as possible when you are working outside. You won't be able to do your best if you are uncomfortable or balanced precariously.

Although this was a simple sketch, I had to think carefully and really observe my subject as I worked. When drawing a scene like the estuary, it wouldn't be too noticeable if a field or a tree was put in the wrong place. However, if a mast is badly positioned, it will look wrong! I drew the hull first and then positioned the mast, which helped me to position the blue canopy. Then I drew a line for the furthest bank before adding some shading and a little detail.

If you aren't familiar with a subject like this and want to work from your sketch at home, you will also need to take a photograph from your sitting position. I did my painting in the studio on cartridge paper, 20 x 28 cm (8 x 11 in). I didn't work over the original sketch; I drew it again. I painted the sky first, then worked the yellow of the clouds and, while it was wet, added a shadow colour to it which merged the colours. I then painted in the blue sky above the clouds and this gave them their shape. I continued under the main clouds with horizontal brush strokes, adding green as I went over the land.

I had to wait for the sky to dry before I worked on the yacht. Notice how dark the white hull is, especially at the bows. This helps it to stand out against the light blue of the water. The water was painted with horizontal brush strokes and any underpainting or paper that shows through gives the impression of water movement (see the demonstration photograph on the previous page). The rigging and grasses on the bank were done with my rigger brush.

IMPORTANT COLOURS

The clouds
Yellow Ochre

The cloud shadows
French Ultramarine and a touch of Crimson Alizarin, allowed to mix with wet cloud colour

The canopy
French Ultramarine

The yacht hull
French Ultramarine, a touch of Crimson Alizarin and Yellow Ochre

Watercolour on cartridge, 20 x 28 cm (8 x 11 in)

This yacht really whetted my artistic appetite!

PAINTING TIPS

Have your paper at an angle to allow the paint to run down

To create a hard edge, you must paint over dry paint. If you paint on wet paint, the paint will run and mix together, creating a soft edge

It is tempting to fiddle when you use a small brush for detail work. Discipline yourself not to do this!

CLOSE-UP DETAILS

▶ To create the softness of the cloud, I painted the yellow first, and then I added the cloud shadow colour to it while it was still wet. This allowed the colours to run and blend together

▶ I used the blue sky colour to suggest puddles of water and allowed the path colour to run into it in places while it was still wet (see also the autumn painting on page 25). I haven't put any detail into the foreground, but the free brush strokes are painted in perspective, giving the impression that the path is flat

▲ I made sure the sky was dry before painting the blue canopy. This enabled me to get a crisp edge to it. Look how freely I painted the rigging with my rigger brush. The light-coloured rails and supports on the deck were achieved by painting the dark colours around them

▲ The yacht hull stands out from the background because it is painted dark against the light-coloured water and distant bank

▶ Notice how simply the distant clouds and landscape are painted. This simplicity helps to keep it all in the background. In a free-style painting like this, try not to overwork areas as this will spoil your painting. The thin rushes and grasses were painted with my rigger brush

PROGRAMME

3

USING PHOTOGRAPHS

PEN AND WASH

A photograph is one of the best sources of information and inspiration when you are in the studio. Don't worry – there is nothing wrong with copying photographs, as long as you don't assume that they can take the place of nature. Of course, there are people who cannot get out and about to paint and I have met many artists for whom photographs are a prime source of information and who paint fabulous pictures. However, working directly from nature when you can will help you to understand your photographs and to paint better pictures from them. Whether you paint from just a photograph or use a photograph with a sketch, here are some useful points to bear in mind.

1 Whenever possible, take your own photographs. This means that you will have experienced the scene yourself and you'll be amazed at how much will come flooding back when you start to work from the photograph.

2 Take slides if possible. If you have a projector, you can enlarge these onto a screen and almost 'relive' the scene before you start to paint. Naturally, you will need a small viewer to work from while you are painting.

3 Remember that colours can become distorted in a photograph so don't try to copy them too slavishly. You are creating a painting, not recreating the photograph!

4 If you are using a sketch to work from as well as a photograph, then copy your sketch for the drawing, not the photograph. Use the photograph as an aide mémoire to help fill in the gaps.

5 Try doing a pencil sketch outside and also taking a photograph from your sketching position. If you compare the two when the photograph is developed, you will see the difference between what the camera saw and what you saw. This is a very important exercise and, believe me, you will learn a lot from it.

6 You don't have to copy all the photograph. A small section of it could make a painting. In the last programme, I sketched a small section of the estuary rather than the whole of the scene in front of me. Look at some of your old photographs with this in mind. You could find some exciting new 'paintings'.

7 Always remember that, whatever the subject, the photograph is there to give you information and it may also give you inspiration. However, you are not trying to create a large photograph and so you must apply your own creative talents to your painting as well. Keep this uppermost in your mind when you are working and you will create a good painting – it could even turn out to be a masterpiece!

For this programme, I worked from a photograph using pen and wash. This is a lovely medium to work with because you can paint as freely as you like, knowing that the pen, when worked over the watercolour 'painting', will make the final important shapes.

ABOVE How many times do we take a photograph looking into the sun? A photograph like the one above is usually the result! You can work from a photograph like this, but it will have to be painted in silhouette. Don't make the buildings or the gondolas as black as they appear in the photo, though

BELOW: This silhouette photograph gives me a tremendous feeling of atmosphere. I would really enjoy painting a picture from this

TOP RIGHT: A better photograph still! This would make a lovely, delicate watercolour

ABOVE: I photographed this balcony on one of my painting holidays and it's a subject that would work very well in pen and wash. I would have done a sketch of it but there just wasn't time. This is when a camera is invaluable to the artist. If you can't paint it, capture it on camera to use when you are back at home

I used this photograph for the programme

The scene above inspired me when my wife June and I were on a Greek island with a group of painting students. I had no time to sketch it, and so I took the photograph.

I used the photograph for my demonstration in this television programme. The producer loved it because it had a different subject matter to my normal landscapes, but he was a little concerned about doing it live in front of the cameras. He saw the photograph as a very complicated and difficult scene. On the other hand, I was looking at the photograph and turning it into a painting in my mind's eye. I was imagining doing it in pen and wash, and could already see my pen dancing around the figures. So I said, very confidently, 'Don't worry, David, I can do it for you,' before I even realised the challenge I had set myself!

I didn't look at the photograph with a view to making a perfect copy of it – as I said earlier, you're creating a painting, not recreating a photograph. Even so, if drawing isn't your strong point, this picture could be a little ambitious for you to begin with. If it is, try copying a simpler photograph but still work in pen and wash.

One of the reasons I like pen and wash is that you can apply the watercolour (before you draw over it with the pen) in a very free and unlaboured way. It doesn't matter if the colours run together since it is really the pen that makes the final definition between shapes.

Usually you work on a paper or board with a hard, smooth surface. This enables the pen to move over it easily. Because of this surface, the watercolour runs over it, rather than sinking in to it. This makes working wet paint into wet very exciting, especially when you can tidy up the unpredictable shapes when it is dry with your pen. If you look at the example below, you can see how the paint has run and mixed – it happens very quickly on this type of paper.

I did the painting on the opposite page after drawing it first with a 2B pencil. I started painting at the top, gradually working down the paper. I was reasonably careful when painting the windows on the ship, but my brush strokes were still quite free. Notice how simply I painted the symbol on the funnel and the lifeboat below it. When you work in a free style like this, you must keep the same feeling throughout the painting. If you are going to be

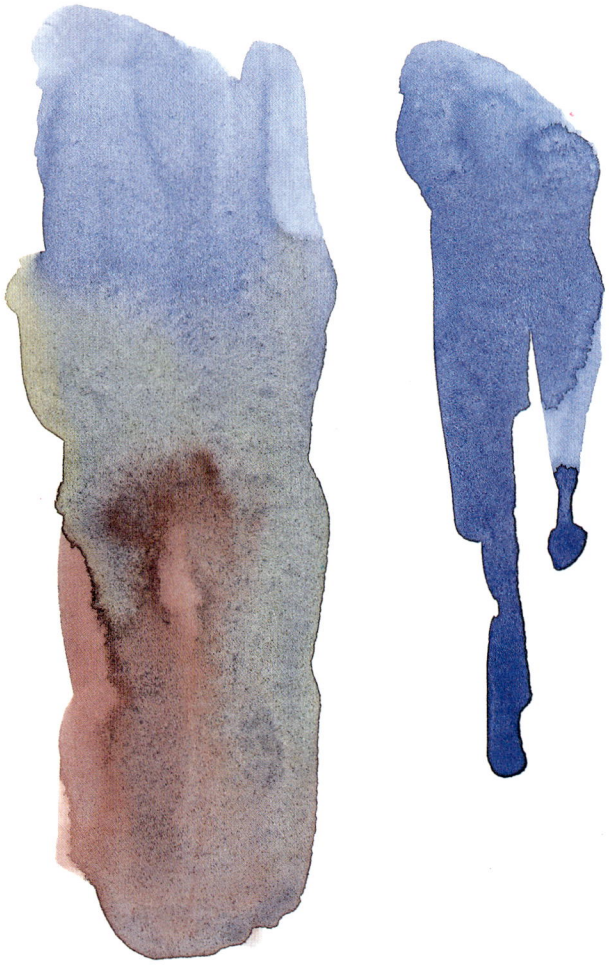

Watercolour applied very wet on Ivorex Board

Watercolour on Ivorex Board before pen and ink was used, 30 x 38 cm (12 x 15 in)

more precise anywhere, it should be the centre of interest or focal point that deserves more careful definition.

I didn't paint the sky as strong in colour as it was in the photograph or put in the flagpole on the right of the picture. I also left out some of the people in the foreground because I didn't feel they helped the composition. Observe how simply I painted the two boats on the left. The brush strokes on the quay are painted in perspective and this helps the quay to look flat and gives the illusion of it going away from us. The shadows of the people are also very important for exactly the same reason.

Examine the painting again. This is as far as I went with watercolour before I started to work with my pen. Now turn to the next page to see what happened when I did.

> **IMPORTANT COLOURS**
>
> **The sky and sea**
> French Ultramarine, Crimson Alizarin and a touch of Yellow Ochre
>
> **The quay**
> Yellow Ochre, Crimson Alizarin and a touch of French Ultramarine

PROGRAMME THREE

When you're drawing with ink you must use waterproof ink. Since this isn't soluble in water, if you wish to add more colour over the ink when it is dry, it will not run.

Hold the pen in the same way that you would to write with (see the photo, below right). When you make an upward pen stroke, take the pressure off slightly or the nib could catch in the paper, splattering the ink. Incidentally, some artists do this on purpose to give a little more technique to the painting. When you want a thicker line, put pressure on the nib and use a downward stroke. Practise on some spare paper or board and you will soon get used to what the pen can do.

I find that the secret of using the pen is to move it quickly over the painting. Don't try to 'draw' everything in carefully. When I drew over the people in the middle of the painting with ink, June, who was watching what I was doing on the TV monitor, said it looked as though it had been speeded up; the pen moved about so quickly.

You have to be sure of what you are painting to be able to do this, and your brain must always co-ordinate with your pen. Let me explain.

When the pen is working on the people, I am 'thinking people'. The human body has softness and mobility and the pen strokes should be very free to give this effect. The lines don't have to marry exactly with the painted area, or you would end up with a painting that looked like an outline drawing that had been filled in with colour. If you 'think people', you will know that, if you start at the head, there will be a body with arms and legs underneath, so you won't have to think where your pen has to go or what it has to do to form the shape. If this sounds too far-fetched, try it. I know you will be convinced – but it does need practice.

The detail below has been enlarged twice the size that I drew it to show you just how free the pen strokes are. In a scene like this, we want to give an impression of a group of people, not a portrait gallery! I didn't do any pen work on the quay; it would have made it too fussy.

Finally, there are no rules as to how much or how little pen or wash you use in a painting; it's up to the individual artist. So why not have a go? It really is easier than you think!

Detail from my painting opposite, reproduced twice the size it was painted

Pen and wash on Ivorex Board 30 x 38 cm (12 x 15 in)

▲ The painting before pen and ink was used

▶ Hold your pen as you would for writing

41

CLOSE-UP DETAILS

▶ See how simply the ship's symbol and the lifeboat are painted. There is very little penwork since this would make the lifeboat too prominent

▶ Although the 'windows' were carefully positioned, the brush strokes that made them were applied freely. Make sure this freedom runs through your painting. When I was working over the painting with my pen, I squared the windows up slightly with pen lines

▲ You can see how the paint of the orange-coloured barrier ran into the quayside colour. Let this 'colour-mixing' happen. The shape was later defined by the pen and ink

▲ The red boat is painted so freely that it hardly looks like a boat. I only put a couple of pen lines on it but that was enough – I didn't want the eye to be drawn to it. The painting is about a group of people coming off a ship, and this is where the emphasis has got to be

▶ I painted round the white awning posts on the stern with blue sea colour. They are painted as freely as the red boat. After we had finished filming this programme, I spotted a mistake! If you look at the stern, you will see what appear to be three white panels. Actually, these are spaces between supports, and should have been painted as blue sea. I promise to do better next time!

PROGRAMME

4

PAINTING SKIES

I don't think there's a better watercolour subject than skies for working in the studio. It's also one of the best subjects for practising watercolour. This is because, to paint skies, you don't need to concentrate on doing complicated drawings and the colours you'll use are reasonably easy to mix. You can also create skies out of your imagination and they will look good. Finally, you will have the opportunity to use broad washes of paint. This is very exciting to do, and you will learn a lot. You can work wet-on-wet, wet-on-dry – or a mixture of both – with a spontaneous freedom and virtually no restriction. In other words, the sky's the limit!

I gained much of my experience of colour mixing and applying washes in this way when I was at art school. Naturally you must have a little knowledge about the sky, but you can keep your feet firmly planted on the earth to do it!

The best way to start is to do pencil sketches of the sky, using pencil-shading instead of colour. This makes the sketching much quicker, and this helps when the clouds are moving fast. There are many skies that are almost impossible to paint from life, even for professional artists. This is simply because the mood or the shapes are only there for minutes. Watch how often a cloudy sunset changes in the last hour before sundown. You could see ten or even fifteen different skies! This is where a camera is very useful. But you must observe skies and work from them, too. Don't just rely on photographs.

When we were making this programme, we saw some fabulous skies. One day, small clouds were moving quite quickly across a deep blue sky and, for a while, it looked just like a painted

This sky looks just like a painted wash

watercolour wash (see above). The wispy cloud at the bottom is real, which helps to give scale. This is the simplest-looking sky you can paint, though not, incidentally, the easiest!

First, you have to master painting a wash. Your board must be at an angle and the secret of applying a wash is to mix plenty of watery paint in your palette and load your largest brush with it. Always start at the top left-hand side of the paper, taking the brush along in a wide, even stroke. When you reach the end of the stroke, simply lift the brush off the paper, bring it back to the beginning and start another stroke, running along the bottom of the last wet stroke (see the demonstration photo, below right).

Watercolour on Waterford 300 lb Not, 28 × 38 cm (11 × 15 in)

Continue down the paper in this way. In the painting above, I changed the colour as I worked down the paper to give an evening sky effect. When you paint a sky, even if you're just practising, put a suggestion of a landscape at the bottom. This will give your sky depth, scale and realism – it brings a simple wash to life! Try it.

IMPORTANT COLOURS
Evening sky
French Ultramarine with Yellow Ochre, adding Crimson Alizarin and more Yellow Ochre

▶ When painting a wash, take your fully-loaded brush along in wide, even strokes

Detail from my painting opposite, reproduced actual size

The sky on the opposite page shows another way of painting a wash. I did the one on page 45 on dry paper, but for this wash I worked wet-on-wet. This simply means that you are painting wet paint onto (and into) more wet paint. Remember, when you work this way, you will always have the paint running and mixing together, and so you won't have any hard edges.

The detail, left, is a section of the stormy sky painting on the opposite page, reproduced actual size. I mixed the colours I wanted in my palette first. Then I wet the paper all over, except for the bottom right-hand corner, where the house and tree were to be. Always mix your colours first, or your paper could be dry by the time you are ready to start. I wanted to get a 'rain effect' and I achieved this by working the brush in vertical strokes (see demonstration photo, below right), not horizontal ones as in the previous wash. At the top right of my painting, I added more water which made the pigment weaker. You can see how the pigment ran down from above, to give the illusion of rain. This happened half-way down the sky, when I added more Yellow Ochre to the wash, then more French Ultramarine and finally more water as it ran into the land.

The brightness at the bottom right of the painting was achieved by **not** wetting this area. This meant that, when the wash ran down the paper, it stopped where the paper was dry.

This wet-on-wet technique is a fabulous way of experimenting with skies and, of course, watercolour in general. I know you will want to paint lots of skies once you get caught up in the excitement of it – and that should be after just one or two attempts! Because of this, you could find yourself using a lot of watercolour paper. Cartridge drawing paper is less costly and I use it a lot for sizes up to 28 cm x 40 cm (11 x 16 in). One of the skies on page 49 was done on this type of paper.

IMPORTANT COLOURS
The stormy sky
French Ultramarine, Yellow Ochre and a little Crimson Alizarin

Watercolour on Bockingford 200lb, 28 x 38 cm (11 x 15 in)

▶ To get a 'rain' effect, work the brush in vertical strokes

Watercolour on grey-tinted Bockingford 140 lb, 28 x 38 cm (11 x 15 in)

Another exciting way of painting skies is to use tinted paper. In this programme, I used grey-tinted Bockingford watercolour paper to show the contrast with paintings I had already done on cream-tinted and cartridge paper (white). You can compare all three paintings on these pages. The two on tinted paper were painted with the same colours, although it was impossible to match the density and tonal values exactly since they were done at separate times.

The most important part of this exercise was to show how working on a colour unifies a painting and can give it a particular atmosphere. The sky on cream paper has a warm evening glow to it, while the sky on grey paper has a cool and almost damp early morning atmosphere.

I painted the early morning sky, above, starting as usual at the top and working down. After painting the blue of the sky, I worked in some Yellow Ochre for the clouds, and I let it touch the blue in places where it mixed and softened the edges. I left some areas of unpainted paper and then added shadows on the underside of the main clouds. As the paint was still wet, the shadow colour ran back up into the clouds.

I then painted across the sky underneath the main clouds and worked down and over the horizon. You will see that, where I let this wash touch the bottom of the wet clouds, the colours have merged together. I didn't paint the river; I left it as unpainted paper. When the sky was dry, I painted over the horizon to suggest fields, making a silhouette against the morning sky. I also suggested two small figures in the foreground to give scale.

You will notice that the sky on cartridge paper, opposite, has areas under the clouds where the paint has run back on itself and formed what artists call a 'cauliflower'. This does happen on cartridge paper, but don't let it worry you – this is part of its character. If you don't like it, use watercolour paper.

Watercolour on cream-tinted Bockingford 140 lb, 28 x 38 cm (11 x 15 in)

Watercolour on cartridge paper, 20 x 28 cm (8 x 11 in)

• PROGRAMME FOUR •

Film processing can sometimes make a sky photo too 'blue'

I painted the sky on the opposite page while being filmed. You will immediately notice that there is one very important difference between my painting and the photograph, above, which is of a similar sky. The photograph has made the clouds look very cold and blue. This colouring was untrue to real life and this is something that can happen in photographic processing. However, I made sure that my painting had a lot of warmth in the clouds and that they looked more colourful and lively. This is something you must aim for, especially when you work from a photograph.

I painted this sky in exactly the same way as I'd painted the two on tinted paper previously. However, this time I painted on a 'rough' surface paper and you can see how the texture helps to give a lively effect to the clouds.

Two important brush strokes that I use constantly for sky painting are shown opposite. Fig. A illustrates how I worked the blue sky at the top of the painting by dragging my brush across the paper. Although my brush was loaded with watery paint, because the paper was rough, the stroke becomes rather 'hit-and-miss' in places, giving a lovely broken edge similar to a dry brush stroke. If you flatten the brush hairs with a slight pressure, you'll find you can make the paint stop flowing when you want it to. This needs practice, but it's well worth the time and effort.

Fig. B shows the brush stroke I used for the clouds. By dragging the brush horizontally and vertically, even against the 'grain', you'll find the brush will break away from the surface, and touch again, leaving exciting cloud shapes. Practise this – once you've mastered it, your cloudy skies will improve by a hundred per cent!

Most of the skies that you paint will have clouds, some cloud shadows and blue sky. Below, as a general guide, are the important colours to use when painting skies.

IMPORTANT COLOURS

The blue sky
French Ultramarine and Crimson Alizarin, adding more Crimson Alizarin and a touch of Yellow Ochre towards the horizon

The clouds
Yellow Ochre and unpainted paper

The cloud shadows
French Ultramarine, a touch of Crimson Alizarin and Yellow Ochre

Watercolour on Whatman 200 lb Rough, 28 x 38 cm (11 x 15 in)

Fig. A

Fig. B

- Once you start a sky, you must continue and finish it in one operation while the paint is wet, or your colours won't mix together

- I painted the sky almost to the bottom of the paper and this is very important. Where the paint was left showing through to represent fields, these fields reflect the sky colour. This helps to unify the sky and the land and, therefore, unifies the painting

- All the skies in this programme were painted with just one 'wash'. If you want to, you can always work over a sky when it is dry to add more depth and detail

▶ Watercolour on Whatman 200 lb Rough, reproduced actual size

PAINTING TIPS

Use bags of water when you paint a cloudy sky so that your colours run and merge together

When painting a sky study, paint in some land to give scale to the sky

Always mix enough colour for a wash or, by the time you have mixed some more, the wash may be too dry to continue

PROGRAMME 5

USING IMAGINATION

You really can let your creative genius run wild when you work from imagination in the studio! You can create a world of your own and, because you are working at home, you can do it in comfort and in your own time. When I create a landscape from imagination, I really do get lost in it – in fact, I thoroughly enjoy every minute, from drawing it in pencil to the very last brush stroke. Naturally, I have paintings that go wrong or that I am not happy with, but I still get tremendous pleasure from the actual creation and painting of the scene, irrespective of the result.

If you were painting an imaginary scene of a distant planet in a far-off galaxy, then that would be pure imagination, because you could never have witnessed such a scene. But when you paint a landscape from imagination, you are relying on your memory as well as your imagination. After all, you know what a tree looks like, or a field, a sky, a hedgerow, and so on. Therefore, as you create the scene, your imagination is fed by your memory. This means, of course, that the more sketching you have done from nature, the easier it will be for you. If you are unable to do much sketching outside, then your knowledge will come from photographs, books and television.

I often find when I paint from imagination that I create a landscape with which I am very familiar – usually from within my local area. Try to imagine a scene on your paper before you start to draw. If you want to, draw some small, quick sketches in pencil on cartridge paper to get your imagination working. These can be as complicated or as simple as you like. You may find you only need to do one, but on other occasions you could do ten or fifteen before you are satisfied. Then copy the sketch on to the paper on which you are going to paint.

This exercise in itself is very rewarding. Once you have created your landscape, if you feel you need more information for a tree, for instance, then you could work from a pencil sketch you have previously done, or from a photograph you have taken. A painting done from imagination could even be created from a combination of memory, old sketches, photographs, television images and books.

I wanted to paint a snow scene for this programme and started by doing the two pencil sketches opposite. I decided the top sketch didn't have enough foreground to give prominence to the snow and, although I liked the composition of the one below, I felt that again there wasn't enough snow area in it. My next pencil sketch, shown at the top of page 56, had too much snow and the scene was not intimate enough. Also, the trees and people were too far away. My final one, shown below it, was just what my imagination was looking for. There was enough foreground to show snow, the trees were reasonably close and the figures were large enough to be of importance.

▶ 2B pencil on cartridge paper, reproduced actual size

• PROGRAMME FIVE •

PROGRAMME FIVE

Watercolour on Whatman 200 lb Rough, 38 x 50 cm (15 x 20 in)

Incidentally, the other three scenes are just as good as the one I used, and I may use them all in the future if (and this is very important) they capture my imagination at another time. You must be completely confident that you want to paint the scene you have created. If not, continue to create other ones until you have got what you want. You will find that your sixth sense tells you when you get it right.

When you paint from imagination, you must always keep the mood or atmosphere that you wish to give to your painting uppermost in your mind. You can't observe this in the same way that you could if you were working outdoors. Instead, try to imagine a day when you experienced the mood that you are trying to capture. Then keep referring to this picture in your mind's eye as you work.

When you paint snow in watercolour, the secret is to leave as much white paper as possible to represent snow. However, to make it look more realistic, you must put some tonal work into it to give form and shape. Also add some mud or grasses breaking through the snow in places because this also helps to give form.

IMPORTANT COLOURS

The snow
White paper

The snow shadows
French Ultramarine, a little Crimson Alizarin and a touch of Yellow Ochre

The dark tree
French Ultramarine, Crimson Alizarin, Hooker's Green No. 1 and a touch of Yellow Ochre

The light tree
Yellow Ochre, Crimson Alizarin, Hooker's Green No. 1 and a touch of French Ultramarine

CLOSE-UP DETAILS

▶ The small branches were painted with my rigger brush

▼ This shows how free you can be with the tonal work on snow. Use these tones to show the contour of the ground. I used the same brush stroke as I used for clouds – notice how the dry brush work helps to make the snow sparkle

▲ I allowed the paint on the figures to run together. This helps to soften them and keep them in the middle distance

▲ I left small areas of paper unpainted on the branches. This helps to give the illusion of snow

▶ The distant fields were created with hedgerows and trees using the same colours as the snow shadows (but at times a little darker). Notice how the fields become narrower as they recede to the horizon

PROGRAMME

6

CREATING ATMOSPHERE

In Programme One, I drew one pencil sketch and used it in the studio to paint different seasons. For this programme, I did one pencil sketch but this time I used it to paint different atmospheres. I did the sketch on my local beach in Dawlish, where there is a very distinct headland. I worked standing for technical reasons but if you can sit down it is easier. Your pencil lines will be more definite because you can rest your pad on your knees, and you will be in a more comfortable position for sketching.

The first and most important pencil line on a sketch for a seascape is the horizon: this must be parallel to the top and bottom of your paper. I then positioned the main rocks and headland, and worked my way down the sketch. When two people passed by the rocks, I sketched them in to give scale to that part of the beach. This is important and it gave life to the scene.

In the programme, I showed how versatile a pencil can be. Use a 2B pencil for sketching and sharpen it with a knife, not a pencil sharpener. You can create a long pencil lead with a sharp knife, and you will need this to enable you to get the most out of your pencil. Don't be afraid to put pressure on to get dark tones, or to take pressure off the lead to create light tones (see my demonstration photograph). As the pencil point wears down you will get a thick line but, if you turn the pencil half-round and draw on the flat part of the lead, you can draw a very thin line. Practise on a scrap of paper. When you can control your pencil, you will create better sketches and enjoy sketching more.

Trying to decide what atmosphere to paint at home is very similar to working from your

The view of the headland from Dawlish beach

imagination. The way I do it is to sit quietly and think of different times that really stand out in my memory. It could be a day when I've started out early and a cold mist has drifted over the countryside, or a very hot day with strong shadows breaking up the sunlight. That's the beauty of our memory – it stores up visual experiences to use at a later date, although sometimes they need a trigger to bring them to the surface.

Another way of finding atmosphere is to look at some of your photographs because these can often give you inspiration. If you remember, I said that one of the silhouette photographss on page 37 gave me a tremendous feeling of atmosphere. On another day, I could be inspired by a photograph I had previously rejected. It all depends how you are feeling – on some days you will feel like painting something very delicate and, on others, something very bold and strong. When you are in the studio, the decision is yours!

• PROGRAMME SIX •

2B pencil on cartridge paper, 20 x 28 cm (8 x 11 in)

▲ Sketching for the television programme

▶ When sketching with pencil, put pressure on the lead to get dark tones and take pressure off to create light tones

2B pencil on cartridge paper, reproduced actual size

LATE AFTERNOON

As I said in Programme Four, you can draw some very simple, small sketches in pencil to give you a tonal 'feel' for a painting. The one I did for this programme (above) was sketched very freely and without any concern for detailed shapes. I just wanted to show you and the viewers what was in my mind's eye – the dark cliffs against a bright sky background. I imagined a late autumn afternoon, when the wind had dropped and the atmosphere was ideal for a brisk walk on the beach.

Sometimes a small pencil sketch comes first and, as you 'doodle', you will find yourself putting atmosphere into it. At other times, the atmosphere will inspire you first and then, if you feel you want to sketch in the tonal work before you start, that's fine.

Remember, we are all different and so our creative thinking does not necessarily follow exactly the same pattern as the next person's. Whichever way you find the most rewarding and enjoyable should be the way for you.

When you copy your sketch on to watercolour paper, the most important line is the horizon, just as it was with your sketch. When I painted the sky, I continued down the painting and into the sea with horizontal brush strokes, leaving some unpainted paper to represent sunlit water and waves. I waited for the sky to dry before I painted the distant headland, local cliffs and rocks. The beach was done with three washes, and I let each one dry before the next was applied. Looking at the painting now, I wish I had left some horizontal highlights on the cliff's reflection on the beach. Apart from that, I'm happy with it.

• PROGRAMME SIX •

Watercolour on Waterford 300 lb Rough, 28 x 38 cm (11 x 15 in)

IMPORTANT COLOURS

The sky
Mainly Yellow Ochre and Crimson Alizarin, with a touch of French Ultramarine

The cliffs
Crimson Alizarin, a little French Ultramarine and Hooker's Green No. 1

The beach
The same colours as the sky, with more Crimson Alizarin and French Ultramarine added

2B pencil on cartridge paper, reproduced actual size

BEFORE THE STORM

This painting has a very powerful atmosphere. It's the quiet, still period before a storm. The sun is still out behind and to the left of where I did the sketch and it has flooded the cliffs with a ghostly light. The calm sea appears to be a dull silver against the dark, forbidding sky. We only get glimpses of nature in these moods, because they don't last very long. In fact, a scene like this would be totally different half an hour later. When you are lucky enough to be in the right place at the right time to witness a breathtaking gem of nature, look at it and observe it for future reference. If you do happen to have a sketch book with you, quickly sketch the important elements.

For instance, the shape of the rocks and cliffs are not as important as the dark sky and light-coloured water. No matter how free and undetailed the sketch is because of speed, it will have made you look and observe, and that information will stay in your memory. Naturally, if you have your camera with you, it's even better. You will have the scene and its atmosphere captured forever.

If I had been on the beach, I would have done a quick sketch no different to the one above, which shows the important elements needed to capture the atmosphere. But remember, it would work for me. Someone else may need more or less information.

I painted the dark sky first, working around the cliffs. When this was dry, I painted the distant headland, cliffs, rocks and the beach. I left the sea as unpainted paper.

When all this was dry, I decided to make the sky even darker still. I gave it another wash and continued this down over the distant headland, the horizon and into the sea. This final wash gave me the depth of colour I wanted.

On this type of paper, I was able to wipe out the two figures with a damp brush (see below right). They look very ghostly, don't they?

Watercolour on Bockingford 200 lb, 28 x 38 cm (11 x 15 in)

IMPORTANT COLOURS

The sky
French Ultramarine, Yellow Ochre and Crimson Alizarin. More Yellow Ochre was added nearer the horizon

The cliffs
Yellow Ochre, Crimson Alizarin, Hooker's Green No. 1 and a little French Ultramarine

▶ I used a damp brush to wipe out the figures

In the Mist

The atmosphere I decided to create for my next painting on television was a misty day. A sea mist adds a 'fairytale' look to a painting, bringing an air of mystery to the scene. Like a stormy atmosphere, it can be difficult to sketch on the spot. I have been on a beach where the mist has come down in minutes and, just when you think it is there forever, it can disappear in minutes. So, once again, you have the problem of being in the right place at the right time, with your sketchbook and your camera. I suppose the easiest atmosphere to find and paint on location is a sunny, cloudy day and, depending on the subject, this can be just as exciting as some of the more 'artistically romantic' atmospheres.

There are two different ways of painting the effect of mist in watercolour. One method is to work wet-on-wet, allowing the colours to run together and create a soft, misty look. You are not always in complete control of the paint when using this method but you can get some very interesting 'happy accidents'. For this particular painting, however, I worked wash-over-wash, painting each new wash when the previous one was dry. It is a more controlled way of working and I had to be in control of the paint under the television cameras!

I painted the sky first and worked it down behind the cliffs and into the sea. When this was dry, I painted the cliffs and, when the cliffs were dry, I painted over the nearest cliff with a darker, warmer colour.

I painted the rocks that were still uncovered by the sea and painted round the two figures on the beach. Because this paper is not as good as the previous paper for wiping out, I worked the beach in two simple washes and, when these were dry, I painted in the reflections of the cliffs. Notice how the dark rocks going into the sea help to make the light colour of the cliffs and the mist lighter by contrast.

Creating atmosphere at home can be very exciting and rewarding. It also gives you a reason to experiment with paint, ideas, and your own imagination and memory.

Filming in my studio

PAINTING TIPS

Remember that, with watercolour, the whitest part of your painting is the paper. If you want something to be 'white paper', you must paint round it all through the painting process, as I did with the figures in the painting opposite

Although some watercolour papers will allow lifting out or wiping out with a damp brush or blotting paper, it will never come out as white as the paper

Don't fiddle!

• PROGRAMME SIX •

Watercolour on Waterford 300 lb Rough, 28 x 38 cm (11 x 15 in)

IMPORTANT COLOURS

The sky and cliffs

A watery wash of French Ultramarine, a little Crimson Alizarin and Yellow Ochre, using less French Ultramarine for the foreground cliffs

The dark rocks

French Ultramarine, Crimson Alizarin and Hooker's Green No. 1

The beach

Yellow Ochre, a touch of Crimson Alizarin and a touch of French Ultramarine

- Always start with a pale wash. I increased the strength as I worked from the horizon down to the foreground rocks

- The delicate, misty look is helped by the strength of the foreground rocks. This dark colour contrasts with the light-coloured background

- The simple brush strokes that suggest a 'tide line' on the bottom right of the beach are important for giving perspective to the beach and the impression of a flat surface

▶ Watercolour on Waterford 300 lb Rough, reproduced actual size

PROGRAMME

IN THE GARDEN

USING GOUACHE

If you have a garden, this can be one of the most convenient places to find inspiration and subjects to paint outside. In the summer, when plants are in full bloom and the weather is warm and dry, you can paint in comfort in many different corners of your garden.

Why not, in the spring and summer, make some pencil sketches and take photographs? It's another exciting way of collecting information to use in the bad weather months. This is what I did for this programme, cheating a little for the sake of television. It was early spring and some flowers were not in bloom, so we went to the local garden centre and bought some ready-grown plants and put them in our garden pots! They made a perfect subject for painting and I was able to sit down to do the sketch, right, which made it easier than some I had done standing up in previous programmes.

The most important aspect of the sketch was to position the three pots in relation to the brick wall. I chose this corner of the garden because the brick wall has character, and leads the eye to the pots from the right of the painting. The two small rocks on the left lead you in from that side and this helps to create a triangular composition. However, if you look at the finished painting in gouache on page 73, you will see that I didn't paint in the thin dark area running up the wall in the centre of the pencil sketch. So the composition has changed to a 'flat' triangle in the finished painting.

When you feel that a painting should differ from a pencil sketch, or it changes during the painting, this is fine.

2B pencil on cartridge paper,

• PROGRAMME SEVEN •

A   B   C   D

On this page, I show you what happens when you paint in gouache on different coloured papers. My first examples, above, are on dark paper. I started with an area of crimson in A with a little water added to the paint (normal working consistency). You can see how well it covers the dark paper. I repeated this next in B, and worked some white paint into it. You can see how the white has mixed and blended with the crimson.

In C, I used thicker white paint first and added a touch of crimson to blend it in. For D, I used more water to paint the crimson area first and, while it was very wet, I put some very watery white in the middle of it and worked some round the side as well. You can see how wet-on-wet in gouache, as in watercolour, gives soft edges. But with gouache it doesn't run into the paint as much as watercolour does. Try experimenting with this – you can get some fabulous effects.

If you look next at E, you will see that I have painted a Yellow Ochre brush stroke. This was normal consistency. Then, with exactly the same colour and consistency, I painted G below it on white paper. The brush stroke on the dark paper appears lighter than the one on the white paper. This is an optical ilusion – light against dark, dark against light. But when I watered the paint down in F, it was darker than H on the white paper below it. This is because the paint has been made thinner by the water and the dark paper is showing through, making the paint duller. The white paper showing through in F is responsible for making the colour lighter.

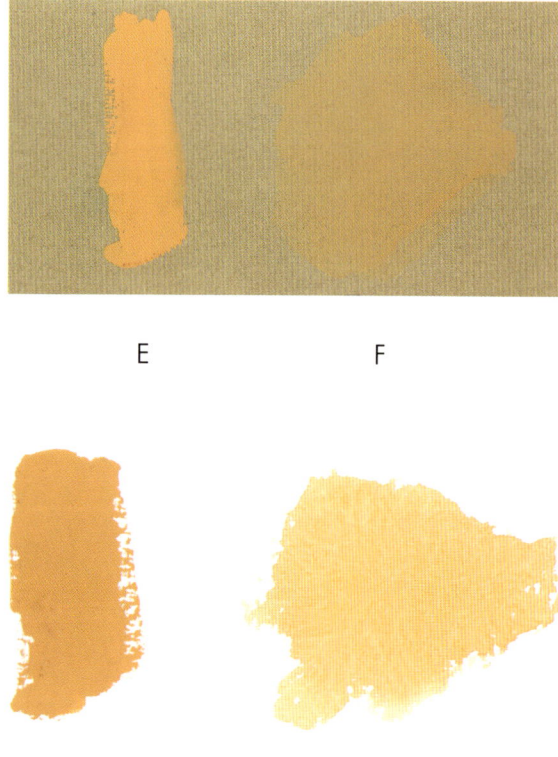

E   F

G   H

You will enjoy working with gouache paint, so do give it a try. There's just one more thing to bear in mind before you start. You will find that, when you work on a dark background, your colours will dry brighter than you anticipated. Remember this as you practise and you'll soon find out just how exciting a medium gouache can be.

Gouache on tan Ingres Board, 20 x 28 cm (8 x 11 in)

IMPORTANT COLOURS

The garden pots and bricks
Cadmium Red, Cadmium Yellow (hue), Permanent White, Yellow Ochre and a little Ultramarine for the shadows

The sunlit leaves
Leaf Green, a touch of Cadmium Yellow (hue) and Permanent White

The white flowers in shadow
Permanent White, a little Ultramarine and a little Crimson

The mauve flowers in shadow
Crimson, Ultramarine and Permanent White

CLOSE-UP DETAILS

▶ The rocks have been suggested by simple brush strokes but the tone and colour were varied. Look how the dark earth makes the orange of the pot look bright (dark against light)

▶ The grey pot helps to break up the orange of the other pots. I painted a simple 'one-brush-stroke' highlight on the rim of the pots – this helps to give the pots more dimension and the feel of dappled sunlight. The bright green leaves were painted after the dark ones. These give the illusion of sunlight falling across them and is in the same bright key as the highlights on the two pots

▲ I used a colour called Geranium for the geraniums with a little white added. Notice how the yellow and mauve flowers are painted in a low key. When I put the lighter colour on, there was enough contrast to make it appear as though the sun was catching them

▲ The white flowers were painted in the same low key (dull, not very bright), and so when I added the white highlights, they looked in shadow, and the brighter paint gave the illusion of sunlight

▶ I painted the bricks first, then added the mortar in between them afterwards. The dark leaves were painted first, and then the lighter ones on top. The colour of the paper is very sympathetic to the subject and I left some showing as part of the painting

PROGRAMME

8

PAINTING LANDSCAPES
USING ACRYLICS

Acrylic is a water-based paint and so I felt it was a good idea to introduce it for the last programme in the series. It is also an excellent medium to use when working indoors. I started painting with it soon after it arrived in this country in 1963 and most of my acrylic painting is done indoors from imagination or using pencil or watercolour sketches done outdoors.

Acrylic paint has some unique qualities, and I think the best way to explain them to you is to compare acrylic to watercolour and oil paint. The paint dries very quickly, but you have to accept this and use it to your advantage. You can choose to paint a picture either with a watercolour technique or an oil painting technique. The paint doesn't smell and you mix water with it to dilute it. To make colours lighter, you add white paint, as in oil and gouache painting, or you add more water, as you do in watercolour.

You can work on a number of surfaces (grounds): canvas, hardboard and almost any paper from watercolour paper down to newspaper. All absorbent surfaces should be primed with an acrylic primer. If you prefer, you can paint directly onto watercolour paper without priming. Cryla Primed Paper is made just for acrylic painting, and I find it ideal to work on. You need a Stay-Wet Palette (shown in the Materials section on page 15), which prevents your paint from drying on the palette. This is a **very important** part of your equipment. You can use hog bristle brushes (as in oil painting), synthetic or sable brushes. Always wash your brushes out in water. Once the paint has dried, it is insoluble in water and your brushes will be ruined. I keep my brushes in a shallow dish of water twenty-four hours a day, seven days a week and still use brushes that have lived like this for many years. You just take the brush out of the dish, dry it on some rag to soak up the excess water and carry on painting. Never keep sable brushes in this way, though, because it could bend the hairs. I wash mine out as I use them, in exactly the same way that I do when I'm working with watercolour.

Getting accustomed to using a Stay-Wet Palette and keeping brushes in water will save on paint, brushes and hours of frustration. If you want to learn more about acrylic painting, my two books: *Learn to Paint Acrylics* and *Alwyn Crawshaw's Acrylic Painting Course* will give you detailed instruction and teach you many ways of painting in this exciting medium.

In Fig. A, you can see what acrylic paint looks like when it is brushed on to a surface. Applied thickly (only use a damp brush), you get texture and the brush strokes remain. If you brush the paint out, the brush strokes will go. Also, the more you brush the paint out, the thinner it will become on the surface and any underpainting will show through. You can buy a medium for mixing with acrylic called Texture Paste. In Fig B, I have mixed paint into it and you can see how thick the mix can be and how it stands out in relief. Texture Paste is white and so when you mix it with colours it will make them paler. However, when it is dry, you can paint over it with darker or lighter colours if you feel it is necessary.

Paint brushed on thickly (impasto)

Paint brushed out (normal painting consistancy)

Paint thinned by brushing out more. This allows underpainting to show through

Fig. A

Paint mixed with texture paste (thick impasto)

Fig. B

PROGRAMME EIGHT

Filming the programme on acrylics for television

If you use a watercolour technique when painting in acrylic, the biggest difference you will find is that, once the paint has dried, it is then insoluble with water. Naturally, this means that, once a colour is dry, you can't mix another colour into it as you can in watercolour painting. However, it does have one advantage. It means that you can paint a wash over a dry wash without fear of pulling up the underwash – something that can make colours muddy, as most of us who paint in watercolour have found out at some time or another to our cost!

In Fig. A, below, I have applied an acrylic wash on watercolour paper in the same way that I applied the watercolour wash on page 45. You can see that I have got a very similar result. This was painted on Bockingford 200 lb paper.

In Fig. B, right, using the same paper, I have painted one wash over another when the previous wash was dry, to demonstrate how you can do this almost indefinitely without previous washes mixing with the newly-applied washes.

This also illustrates how you can build up tone. Each wash was exactly the same as the one before, so the strength of colour or tone depended upon the amounts of washes applied.

Whatever medium you use, there is much to be learned. You need confidence in yourself to get the best results – and confidence only comes from the knowledge of what to expect from your brushes, colours and supports. In turn, this can come from experience gained by practice. But, above all, you must enjoy painting and, believe me, it will show in your work!

Fig. A

Fig. B

I did the painting opposite from imagination, in the same way as the watercolour in Programme Five. I have painted many similar pictures. There are country lanes like this all over the area in which I live and I suppose you could say that my memory played a large part in this particular painting.

I didn't draw a pencil sketch first, but drew directly on to the canvas with my 2B pencil. If you prefer to draw some small pencil sketches first, just as I did in Programme Five, then do so. It was only my experience that enabled me to work directly on to the canvas – but it wasn't always like that for me!

I painted the sky first, and I brushed the paint out because I didn't want thick brush strokes left. This took about five minutes to dry, then I painted the distant trees, using a dry brush technique.

Next I painted the field directly in front of the trees. Notice how I painted the back tree on the right of the picture a warm colour to give the impression of sunlight catching it. I painted this before the main dark tree, so that I could paint its dark branches over the top of it.

The big tree was next. It was worked in a very similar way to the ones I have done in watercolour in previous programmes, except that I used a hog bristle brush for the main trunk. Then I used my No. 6 sable brush for the smaller branches, and finally my rigger brush for the thin branches. When I painted the trunk, I purposely left thick paint on it, to show texture. This helped to give the impression of bark and branches. The feathery branches were created with a hog bristle brush, using a **very** dry brush technique. When you use a sable brush or the rigger for small detail work, you must add enough water to your paint to enable the paint to flow easily from the brush.

When I did the foreground, I painted smaller washes for the puddles just as I would for watercolour painting. When this was dry, I put some small amounts of Texture Paste on the canvas and worked my paint into it. This gave me some texture which helped to create the muddy path. The figures were painted in the same way as I did the watercolour ones in Programme Five, except that the paint didn't run so I had to work it. I still did it with my No. 6 sable brush. When the foreground was dry, I picked out some of the small lumps or light areas of paint and added a shadow to them (on the right side) which gives a three-dimensional look.

I hope this brief introduction to acrylic painting has excited you enough to have a go. I'm sure you will enjoy its versatility, but if you are happy with watercolour and you enjoy painting with it, then carry on being a watercolourist and paint some more masterpieces! I personally enjoy both mediums as much as one another.

IMPORTANT COLOURS

The sky
Titanium White, Ultramarine, Crimson and a little Cadmium Yellow

The big tree
Raw Umber, Bright Green, Crimson and a little Ultramarine, adding white to the colours for the sunlit areas

---

ACRYLIC PAINTING TIPS

Wash your brushes out – keep them in a water dish

Always replace your paint tube tops

Remember that you can paint from dark to light or light to dark. You can use the paint thick (impasto) or thin and watery

• PROGRAMME EIGHT •

Acrylic on canvas, 40 x 30 cm (16 x 12 in)

CLOSE-UP DETAILS

▶ I painted the figures using my No. 6 sable brush. Note that the paint didn't run in the same way that it did when I worked the figures in watercolour in Programme Five

▼ The foreground was created by using Texture Paste and thick paint. The puddles were painted in first with a watercolour technique

▲ These trees were painted using a dry brush technique with a hog bristle brush and an up-and-down brush stroke

▲ I painted the background to this area with a dry brush technique, using a bristle brush. I painted all the branches over this area with my No. 6 sable and rigger brushes

▶ Look at the trunk closely and you will see where I left raised paint to give texture. You can also see the dry brush areas that represent the feathery branches

GALLERY

• G A L L E R Y •

▲ *Winter in the woods.* Watercolour on Bockingford 200 lb, 38 x 50 cm (15 x 20 in)

▼ *A winter river.* Watercolour on Bockingford 200 lb, 38 x 50 cm (15 x 20 in)

PREVIOUS PAGE *A carpet of bluebells.* Watercolour on Bockingford 200 lb, 38 x 50 cm (15 x 20 in)

▶ *Ilkley, Yorkshire.* Watercolour on Bockingford 200 lb, 26 x 19 cm (10½ x 7½ in)

• G A L L E R Y •

▲ *Turf Lock, Devon.* Watercolour on Whatman 200 lb Not, 38 x 50 cm (15 x 20 in)

▲ *The Parson and Clerk, Dawlish, Devon.* Watercolour on Waterford 300 lb Rough
38 x 50 cm (15 x 20 in)

• G A L L E R Y •

▲ *Exmouth Harbour, Devon.*
Watercolour on Whatman 200 lb Not,
38 x 50 cm (15 x 20 in)

▶ *Windy day, River Otter.* Watercolour on
Bockingford 200 lb, 35 x 25 cm (14 x 10 in)

• GALLERY •

▲ *First time round.* Watercolour on Whatman 200 lb Rough, 38 x 50 cm (15 x 20 in)

PREVIOUS PAGE. *Okay, we'll turn back at the gate.* Watercolour on Waterford 300 lb rough, 50 x 80 cm (20 x 32 in)

▲ *An Italian street.* Watercolour on cartridge paper, 22 x 29 cm (8¼ x 11½ in)

• GALLERY •

The rain stopped. Watercolour on Whatman 200 lb Not, 38 x 50 cm (15 x 20 in)

Winter sun. Watercolour on Waterford 300 lb Rough, 38 x 50 cm (15 x 20 in)

• GALLERY •

▲ *Bert and Daisy.*
Watercolour on Whatman
200 lb Not, 19 x 24 cm
(7½ x 9½ in)

◀ *Come on, Daisy.*
Watercolour on
Whatman 200 lb Not,
15 x 19 cm (6 x 7½ in)

▶ *Where's he gone now?*
Watercolour on
Waterford 300 lb Rough,
50 x 38 cm (20 x 15 in)

• GALLERY •

A wonderful view. Acrylic on canvas, 50 x 40 cm (20 x 16 in)